# ITALIAN DAYS & HOURS

# Italian Days & Hours

## Poems by

## Thom Tammaro

ISBN: 9798654567932

Cover photo: "Via Supportici" by Thom Tammaro
Back cover photo: Sheila Coghill
Design and layout: Andrew Jones

Competent Backstop Press
Dubuque, Iowa
www.competentbackstop.com

*per giorni e le ore*

# CONTENTS

*The charm was, as always in Italy, in the tone and the air and the happy hazard of things, which made any positive pretension or claimed importance a comparatively trifling question. We slid, in the steep little place, more or less down hill; we wished, stomachically, we had rather addressed ourselves to a tea-basket; we suffered importunity from unchidden infants who swarmed about our chairs and romped about our feet; we stayed no long time, and "went to see" nothing; yet we communicated to intensity, we lay at our ease in the bosom of the past, we practised intimacy, in short, an intimacy so much greater than the mere accidental and ostensible: the difficulty for the right and grateful expression of which makes the old, the familiar tax on the luxury of loving Italy.*

—Henry James, *Italian Hours*

ITALIAN DAYS & HOURS

# I

*Éie mannate a spassela memoria,*
*è festa*

—Eugenio Cirese

INNOCENT TRAVELER

There was a great storm in the mountains of central Italy that night. Thunder shook the ground, trees trembled, and lightning lit up the sky. Rain fell, unrelenting, for hours, making the steep paths slippery and treacherous. In a farmhouse high above the village, a young woman begged her father and mother to offer her suitor the barn for the night. Reluctantly, they agreed and the young man covered himself in straw, slept dry and safe among barn animals, until morning light.

Coming down the mountain path the next morning, the young man came upon a circle of villagers huddled around the stiff, soaked corpse of a young man. Fingers pointed to bullet holes, one in the side of his head and another just above the heart. The dead man's eyes were wide open until someone forced their lids closed for the last time. Later, the murderer was arrested and confessed to the killing, but said the bullets were meant for the young man who courted the woman who lived in the farmhouse high above the village. Two days later the campanile bells echoed above the village where peasants mourned the tragedy of the innocent traveler.

A few years later, the young man and woman were married, and shortly thereafter boarded a ship in Naples and sailed to America. This was 1907. Their youngest daughter was born in 1924, and nine years later the mother died from a brain tumor. And sometime later, I became the second child of the youngest daughter and her husband.

This afternoon, coming home through the rain, I remember this story and feel the sanctity of my life. How our coming into this world is precarious, our stay tenuous, our going definite. And so I thank the rain. And I thank the barn animals and the straw that kept my grandfather warm and dry through the night. I am even moved to thank the desperate lover and his jealousy. But most of all I thank the innocent traveler coming down the mountain path in the dark, stepping into my life, unaware of what lay ahead in unrelenting rain.

# Found in Translation: My Hotel in Rome

*very ancient hotel ideal for*
*who loves the quiet and*
*great itineraries of history and art,*
*for who feels the breath*
*oh the history!*

# Wide Awake in Rome

Only yesterday morning I stood in the quiet of the
Holy chancel of St. Agostino in San Gimignano

Watching, under bright spotlights, three women
Artisans restoring Benozzo Gozzoli's 15th cent. frescoes

Of the life of St. Agostino, gently painting with tiny brushes,
While listening to taped religious music on a boom box!

But it's Rome, now. 3:00 a.m. And I'm wide awake,
Sitting on the window ledge in the dark

Listening to car doors slamming, taxis honking,
Voices from an Arabian restaurant, music from a disco,

Vespas wasping their way through the streets
And sirens speeding through the Roman night.

I can't seem to locate that quiet space in which
To crawl and sleep at the Hotel Fortunato,

Even though the lucky beggars outside
Termini Station have been dreaming for hours.

At midnight, I went out walking, hoping to tire myself,
But when I lay down the darkness hummed in my ears.

Perhaps I should accept the moment—
The gift my life offers me right now.

Maybe the same God that guided me to St. Agostino
Offers this:

My own exhaustion. The music of my own beating heart.
This whole city below me dissolving into silence.

# ROME, MORNING

Dawn slips through the shutter slats
And across the floor of this tiny room
Where I have slept alone all night.
I get up, pull on my shirt and jeans,
Walk barefoot to the tall window,
Ease open the wooden shutters,
And step out onto the balcony.

Morning bells.
The cooing of pigeons
And the clinking of dishes
From the breakfast room below
Rises in the updraft of the courtyard,
And the wings of starlings beating
Against the humid air.
In the apartment across the courtyard,
A woman stands on her balcony
Combing out her dark hair.
The stone angels of memory
Bow their heads and pray for the lost.

I lean into the quiet morning light,
Warm stone beneath my palms,
Into this ancient rising,
This eternal moment.

# At the Basilica di San Giovanni in Laterano

—Omnium urbis et orbis Ecclesiarum Mater et Caput

Even in the fine dust on the stone floors of cathedrals,
I find the love of the sculptor.

We arrive in the village this afternoon. We are told there was a funeral this morning. A child. Three months old. We do not know how the child died. But it is dead. *Morte.* A sad day for everyone— the mother, the father, relatives and neighbors. Even the priests wept, we are told. Everyone feels sorrow. Three months ago everyone prayed to God to bless the mother and child with strong and healthy lives, but now they pray and ask the same God for mercy, to receive this child in death. Accept him. Protect them. *Preghi per noi.* Pray for us. Everyone in the village is sad on this eve of *festa* Sant' Antonio. Saint of the Poor. Saint of Seekers. Saint of the Lost. Even the fish stopped swimming to listen to him. Tonight the child's father and mother will weep. Will ask for forgiveness from the God who gives and takes. The God they do not understand but fear and love. The God they believe in. The God they curse. The God they beg for forgiveness. The God they embrace. The God they walked away from this morning. The God to whom they will turn to tonight. The God who giveth. The God who taketh away. The God they do not understand. The God they fear. The God they embrace. The God with whom they will live for the rest of their lives in this village we arrived in this afternoon.

# First Morning in Sepino

This morning, I have awakened—
to your morning's brilliant light.
to your mountain's misty slopes.
to your valley's rushing streams.
to the ancient stones of your streets.
to the healing waters of your fountains.
to the chimes of your campanile,
to the red-tiled roofs of your houses.
to your rooster's crow.
to your donkey's bray.
to your cowbells ringing in the pasture.
to your swallow's artful swoop.

Sepino,
you opened your door to let me in,
you embraced me with your heart.

Sepino,
I embrace you in the early morning mist of May.

# Via St. Cristina

This quiet morning,
Walking the narrow
Cobblestone streets
Of the village
With Padre Vittorio,

We watch
A young girl
Approach us,
Holding yellow flowers
In one hand,
In the other
A loaf of bread
Pressed to her side.

Nearing us
She looks up
From the smooth stones
And smiles:
"Pace bene," she says
In a voice warm and bright
As the village sun.

"Pace bene," Padre Vittorio responds.
Indeed, pace bene.

# A SEPINESI FOLK SONG

*Sepino, Sepino, lontano via da voi non sono felice.*
*Sogno di giorni e di notti I di voi.*
*Non faccio niente ma penso voi.*
*Ricordate a me di quando ero un bambino*
*ed a tutto l'amore che lo avete dato.*
*Penso voi notti e giorni,*
*sto pensando sempre voi.*

******

Sepino, Sepino, far away from you I am not happy.
Nights and days I dream of you.
I do nothing but think of you.
You remind me of when I was a child,
and all the love you gave me.
I think of you nights and days,
I am always thinking of you.

## Walking Back to Convento S. S. Trinità on Via Ginnasio

In June
in warm and windy rain
thinking of nothing—
just getting soaked!

FIGS (SEPINO/RAPALLO)

> *"Every fruit has its secret."*
> —D.H. Lawrence, "Figs"

After lunch, Padre Vittorio gets up from the table,
walks outside to the monastery garden and orchard,
comes back with a bowl of figs picked from the tree

we can see through the kitchen window,
washes them in the sink, returns to the table,
and places three fresh figs on each of our plates.

He shows us how to pinch the end and pull
them in half to expose the ruby flesh.
And then we eat. And it's the sweet smell of figs

that reminds me of the evening we left Rapallo
eighteen years ago. We were staying at the Albergo
Moderne e Royale. I think we were the only guests.

We were awakened each morning by the splat of oranges
falling from their trees to the cement walks below us.
We took our morning latté outdoors at a quiet café

along the promenade. A few old men fed pigeons,
and small sailboats moved out into the gulf, disappeared
into the early morning mist of Rapallo.

In the evenings, we strolled alongside women
in gold lamé and watched peddlars offer their cheap wares.
One night we watched a film projected on the side of a building.

Since our train from Rapallo to Genoa didn't depart until
6:00 p.m., we visited the church of Santi Gervasio y Pretasio
and the Leper House of San Lorenzo, then shopped the markets

where we bought *mela, pera, arancia, fragola, uva,* and *fichi*—
apples, pears, oranges, strawberries, grapes, and figs—
and later cheese and bread for the seventeen-hour trip

from Genoa to Amsterdam. In a small shop near the station,
we found antique lace for my mother and later, at a bookstall,
three overpriced paperback novels by Marquez.

When we reached Genoa, we nearly missed our train,
scrambling to board with North African merchants
who stuffed their wares through the train windows.

Near midnight, we shared our figs with a young Italian
literature student who shared our *couchette,* and
in the morning we awoke to the sweet aroma of the figs.

Once, on his way to Jerusalem
with some of his disciples, Jesus was hungry.
In the distance, he saw a fig tree, but when

he discovered it had no fruit, he cursed it
and the tree withered. Later, when he
reached the temple in Jerusalem,

he drove out those money-changers and dove sellers.
Now you know why Jesus was so mad when he
reached the temple in Jerusalem that day.

Mohammed taught that figs are the fruit of paradise.
The naked ripe fruit of heaven pressed against the tongue.

# II

*Ancora imparo.*
—Michelangelo

# SOTTERRANEO



—Michelangelo

I have been keeping my eyes focused on the small wooden door in the southwest corner of the Sagrestia Nuova.  So far, I have seen only one couple emerge from it. No one has gone in.

My ticket is stamped 11:00 a.m., and because it is almost 11:00 a.m., I move toward the wooden door to the left of the chapel where a short, bulky security guard dressed in her neat security blues has been keeping watch, standing and sitting for the past half hour, guarding the door.  And though I've been told that my stamped ticket (stamped because I paid a supplement in addition to the entry fee) will gain me entrance through that door, I have a lingering feeling that it's not going to work. That I'm going to be told "No!  No permesso!" in that same tone I've heard elsewhere in Italy when I've tried to do something I shouldn't be trying to do. In that same tone the waiter used in a restaurant in Venice to tell my wife that she could not have tortellini when she ordered tortellini. We never knew if the restaurant was out of tortellini or if the waiter simply didn't want my wife to have tortellini. We never asked. And so, bewildered, she ordered calamari in sepia ink and later that evening got sick.

But to my surprise—and relief—when I hand the guard my ticket she looks at it, looks back at me, and then opens the door. "Tante grazie," I say to her. "Prego, prego," she says to me. "Attento." She wants me to be careful, and as I step through the doorway I understand why: a narrow metal spiral staircase—wide enough, perhaps, for one person— descends into the light coming from below. I grasp the cold round handrail and begin my descent.

******

*"As for the work, the beginnings are difficult ...."* (1518)

In 1975, during renovations to find another way to deliver tourists to the Sagrestia Nuova—one of the chapels in the great early Renaissance

Basilica of San Lorenzo in Florence—an old custodian remembered a small crypt about the size of a walk-in closet or dorm room, underneath the apse of the chapel. The Sagrestia Nuova—or New Sacristy—is the tomb of two of the lesser Medici family, Lorenzo and Guiliano, cousins of Clement VII, who commissioned Michelangelo to design and build it.

Michelangelo worked on the New Sacristy (named so to distinguish it from Brunelleschi's masterpiece Sagrestia Vecchia or "old sacristy," off the left transept in the main Basilica, thus explaining the name of Michelangelo's sacristy) for fifteen years, though, like so many Michelangelo works, it was never finished.

Michelangelo was forty-five when he accepted the San Lorenzo commission in 1519— his *Pietà*, his *David*, his Sistine ceiling, behind him—and nearly sixty when he abandoned it in 1534, and left for Rome, never to return to Florence except to be placed in his tomb at Santa Croce. I try to imagine a twenty-five-year-old Michelangelo wiping his hands of marble dust on the day he finished the *Pietà*, or a thirty-seven-year-old Michelangelo scraping paint from his hands and clothes on the final day he climbed down from Sistine scaffolds!

******

*"Now I see that it is going to be a long business and I do not know how it will proceed ...."* (1524)

To get to the Michelangelo's New Sacristy, you must enter San Lorenzo through the door off Piazza Madonna degli Aldobrandini, buy your ticket from one of the vendors at the ticket windows, walk through the crypt to the stairs at the back of the church then walk up to the larger chapels of Cappella dei Princini—Chapel of the Princes— a chapel that demonstrates what happens when people have too much money, too much marble, too many semi-precious jewels (enough to cover all of the high walls from floor to ceiling of the octagon-shaped chapel!) and more imagination than taste. But for the frescoes and the sixteen Tuscan coats-of-arms of the Grand Duchy, the Chapel of Princes could be a room in Elvis' Graceland mansion—or at least a room decorated by a distant relative of the Graceland decorator. It is a chapel after Elvis's own heart.

And remember this: when you buy your admission ticket for San Lorenzo, be sure to ask the person at the ticket window for one ticket for the underground Michelangelo drawings: "un biglietto per le illustrazioni sotterranee del Michelangelo, per favore." And then tell no one.

******

*"As for beginning to work, it is necessary to wait for the marbles to come ...."* (1524)

A short hallway leads from the Capella dei Princini to the Sagrestia Nuova, and in just a few short steps, you will receive an unforgettable lesson in art history: Baroque to the Renaissance. You will know, and see, and feel the differences once you step down and into the New Sacristy.

Segrestia Nuova was Michelangelo's first-ever interior architectural design. Remember that Michelangelo, above all, was a sculptor, and so buildings and interior spaces were, for him, nothing more than forms to be sculpted. And the harmonies of the chapel's design illustrate this. One on hand, this is simply a mausoleum, at times austere, cold and damp in its greyish-green marble. On the other hand, the reclining nude allegorical figures of "Dawn," "Dusk," "Night," and "Day" are among the most gorgeous figures Michelangelo ever sculpted out of that most beautiful of marble quarried in Carrara. The figures drape themselves over the tombs, looking as though they are about to slide to the floor—think of liquid mercury spilling from a laboratory beaker. You wait for their chests to rise and fall in breath, their eyes to open, their lips to part—such is the Michelangelo's artistry.

******

*"I am working hard as I can."* (1526)

After nearly five years of preparation, the sotterraneo was opened to the public in 1979. Well, sort of opened to the public. Most of the people who visit San Lorenzo know nothing of the drawings beneath the soles of their feet as they stand in the magnificence of the New Sacristy. And for those who do know, only six-to-eight of them are allowed below at any given time, explaining why no one reads about the sotterraneo in guidebooks. Human traffic would overwhelm the space—and along with it, the thrill of having stumbled onto something few have seen. And then when you are standing there in the midst of the drawings, you will understand why opening up the sotterraneo to the public would require closing it down almost immediately. I would tell you how I found out about it if I could remember. I also realize I am telling you how to find your way there. Now that you know, please do not pass along this secret to anyone. Keep it to yourself.

******

*"I work as much as possible ...."* (1526)

Each step down the spiraling staircase moves you toward the aquarium of light. Reaching the bottom, you find yourself suddenly surrounded by white walls and light. The eyes adjust to the artificial white light that illuminates the space. And then they are drawn in every direction at once, for there is no focal point, unlike most of Michelangelo's designs. This is not architecture, nor painting, nor sculpture. Rather, it is, perhaps, Michelangelo's oversized sketchbook, filled with more than fifty figures and studies sketched in charcoal and red chalk on the walls of a cavern, approximately 26' x 6.6': a nude with right hand on his right thigh and left arm stretched out and above his head as if he's delivering a fastball; upper and lower torsos; legs, standing and striding; a man on his stomach, arms above his head; a reclining woman, her right arm reaching above her head; a crouching man as seen from above; a nude Christ; a seated figure (St. Matthew?) writing; a leg seen from behind; body parts: bent arms, a study of a foot and toes pointing directly toward you; heads; a hand with a finger pointing directly at you.

A short walkway, wide enough for two, moves you from one end of the cavern to the other, metal handrails separating you from the drawings on the walls. If you wanted, you could reach out and trace the drawings with your finger. But the security cameras and alarms would result, most likely, in your arrest and jailing. The climate is controlled, and Plexiglas panels cover the surface of some of the cavern walls to protect the drawings.

******



*"As to the work here, I'll say no more for the moment ...."* (1533)

Siding with the Republic against the exiled Medici, Michelangelo went into hiding in 1530 during the siege of Florence, in fear of reprisals. Indeed, his fears were well-founded: in August of 1530,the temporary Governor of Florence issued an order for Michelangelo's assassination. That is when Michelangelo found his way to the sotterraneo for at least three days, during which he filled the cavern walls with his drawings, using pitch from the torches that provided his light and his own store of red chalk and charcoal sticks. That's one story. There are others, of course. The scholars, ultimately, must determine authenticity and attribution. If you want to read more, locate Caroline Elam's essay "The Mural Drawings in Michelangelo's New Sacristy," or Frederick Hartt's "Michelangelo, the Mural Drawings, and the Medici Chapel," the more thorough and most recent of the studies. Hartt claims that the drawings were made by at least three different people—most of them by Michelangelo, but some by an inept pupil of his, and a few others by a young helper who brought Michelangelo food when he was in hiding. I love the idea of Michelangelo shaking his head as he watches one of his inept students getting the proportion of a hand or leg wrong; or of a young boy bringing Michelangelo a loaf of bread, some cheese and a bottle of wine then asking if he might try drawing on the walls.

******

*"The best of artists never has a concept*
*A single marble block does not contain*
*Inside its husk ...."*

Sotterraneo is a private space. Go there in silence. Take a friend. Better yet, share this experience with someone you love. And then tell no one about it. As it exists now, human traffic will destroy the place. The tombs above, bathed in the muted light from a Pantheon-like oculus, honor the dead in public space. But the true light comes from below.

In private. Sotterraneo honors the living. The life force. The genius mind, fearing for its life. Burning with desire.

******

*"Lord, make me see thy glory in every place."*

# III

*Italy is a dream that keeps returning
for the rest of your life.*
                    —Anna Akhmatova

A Photograph of You at the House of the
Dead in Ascona
              —*for Sheila*


Far from our village on the other side of the hill,
      we found the holy chancel of the Madonna della Fontana.
            We made offerings, lit candles, rested in the shade of

olive trees from the afternoon heat. Later, we found
      the steep stone path our map said would bring us to our
            village in half the time and distance than the road that

brought us here. And it did. Halfway down the hill, we found
      an abandoned chapel. The wooden doors were faded and shut
            tight with a rusty chain and lock. But through the window bars

we counted six pews and a few broken chairs; saw red shards
      of votive candles scattered on a stone floor; smelled
            mildew and rotting boards and dank stone. Against the altar,

two crutches and metal leg braces stood, relics of a fortunate pilgrim.
      And carved in stone above the doorway, a skull and crossbones
            and the words *La Casa della Morte*—the House of the Dead,

where the living come to pray. There in mid-July heat and haze, far above
      Lake Maggiore, we paused in our journey down to the village,
            and I photographed you sitting on the steps of the House of the Dead.

That night, long before the piazza cafés fell silent,
      we fell into bed, exhausted from our pilgrimage.
            Later, we were awakened by the sweet voice of an Italian

tenor singing arias in the hotel lobby three floors below,
      his voice floating like an angel in the cool Swiss night,
            rising to our open window, then drifting above the village

rooftops beyond the bell tower of Santi Pietro e Paolo,
      into the hillsides. And we turned to each other, certain we
            were not dreaming the same dream, remembering our afternoon

searching for the Madonna of the Fountain, descending
the steep stone path, pausing at the House of the Dead,
so full of life and love.

IN ASSISI, AFTER THE QUAKE

> *"…and it would be hard to breathe anywhere an air more
> heavy with holiness."*
>
> —Henry James


1.
I dip my hands and wrists into
the cool water in the stone basin
in front of S. Rufino, hoping to cool myself
from this June morning's blazing sun,
and remember when the ground
quaked once before when Francis stood naked
before his father and renounced the world.

2.
At Santa Chiara, holy Clare, shorn of her
white hair, now kept in a reliquary here,
walked through a door closing it behind
her, reverberating for seven hundred years.

3.
Late afternoon, on the lawn
in front of Basilica di San Francesco
we wander among the white tents—
and the crumbled frescoes
of Cimabue and Giotto.

## JAPANESE WOMAN AT THE CISTERN, PIAZZA DELLA CISTERNA, SAN GIMIGNANO

*Di giugno siati in tale campagnetta*
*che viva sien corbi et arghironcelli*

—Folgòre da San Gimignano

On the bus to San Gimignano, I see its medieval towers long before we reach the town, as they disappear and reappear in the hilly landscape, reminding me of Hemingway describing the bus climbing steadily up Mount Sainte-Victoire in *The Sun Also Rises.* The changing horizon. The shifting perspectives. The sun coming through the trees in patches. Hemingway writing like Cezanne painted.

The gate into the city leads to Piazza del Duomo and the Palazzo del Popolo, where Sala di Dante commemorates his visit in 1300. In Collegiata Cathedral, I find 15th cent. frescoes by Ghirlandaio and Bartolo's *Last Judgment,* a "wonderfully gruesome" painting in which, among other scenes, the devil squats over the face of a usurer and defecates gold coins into his mouth. Leaving the cathedral, I head toward Piazza dell Cisterna and decide to photograph the travertine cistern with the Duomo tower behind it. A Japanese woman stands there and seems not to want to move. I have her in my view finder now, but she doesn't budge. So I try to wait her out—walk to a nearby tabaccheria and buy postcards and stamps, and then return by Viccolo del' Oro, where the goldsmiths hammered sheets of gold into leaf for the artists. When I return, she's still there. Again, I frame her against the cistern, the dark Duomo tower standing tall in the background of the town of fair towers. I try to wait her out. But no luck. I don't think she notices me. I shoot anyway. No horizon. The static perspective. Clouds coming down. The June sun splashing across the piazza.

## Walking to San Miniato al Monte on Sunday Morning

(Via dei Bardi to Via S. Niccolò, through Porta San Miniato
to Via S. Miniato)

Along the way: Andrei Tarkovsy's apartment, Maestro P'rofumiere,
Michaela's Fotografie esclusive di Fierenze in edizione limitata, Busatti
Tessitori in Toccana (dal 1842), Allesandro Dari: Maestro Orafo,
doorway to the Bardini Gardens, M. Tattorini: Antichita, Panni &
Vinni, Cartoleria, il Barreto del Rifrullo, Osteria Antica Mescita, Chiesa
S. Niccolo Sopra Arno and Fabriano's *Quaratesi Polyptych*, Bevvino
Enoteca, il Gelato di Filo, print shops, the balcony of lush flowers with
a della Robbia glazed terracotta roundel, Junka Mukai selling her
miniature watercolor scenes of Florence,

terraced gardens: the secret door to Giardino dell Rose (400 varieties!)
Giardino dell' Iris and a Japanese Garden within, lemon and orange and
olive trees, pilgrims on the wide-terraced stone staircase to Piazzale
Michelangelo who have stopped along the way to catch their breath,
the wall plaque at the intersection of Salvatore al Monte and del Monte
alle Croci where Dante passed on his way to S. Miniato al Monte

PER SALIRE AL MONTE
DOVE SIEDE LA CHIESA CHE SOGGIOGA
LA BEN GUIDATA SOPRA RUBICONTE

SI ROMPE DEL MONTAR I'ARDITA FOGA
LE SCALEE CHE SI FERO AD ETADE
CH'ERA SICURO IL QUADERNO E LA DOGA

DANTE PURGATORIO XII 100-105

the serpentine path to San Miniato al Monte, cherry-flavored Italian
ice against the lips and tongue at Piazzale Michelangelo, mamma gatta
e gattini in their cozy nest beneath a fountain in the olive grove, monks
chanting, the reliquery of St. Minias, il Cimitero delle Porte Sante (the
cemetery of the Holy Doors), the grave of Pinocchio's creator, piercing
cries of ballestrucci, rondoni, rondini, Benedictine honey and liqueurs.

So much along the journey to San Miniato al Monte on Sunday
morning.

# Visiting Pound's Apartment in Venice

*Well, my window…looked out on the Squero where Ogni Santi…*
*meets San Trovaso…things have ends and beginnings.*

          —EP, "Canto LXXVI"


Crawfordsville middle Indiana where I found the wooden door to your apartment
 then a blue plaque at 10 Kensington Church Walk London
  near the station of the Metro 70 Rue Notre Dame des Champs Paris
   the hills of Sant' Ambrogio Casa 60
    the sandy shoreline of Rapallo
And I came here

 861 Rio S. Vio above the bakery
  you ate baked sweet potatoes from street vendors and barley soup.
   watched the changing colors Venetian sun
    almost tossed your poems in the canal
     trying to write paradise
     making it all cohere

and the hidden nest in the dark, narrow —Calle Quierini 252 Dorsoduro Venice

Above your door

IN UN MAI SPENTO AMORE PER VENEZIA
EZRA POUND
TITANO DELLA POESIA
QUESTA CASA ABITO PER MEZZO SECOLO
    COMUNE DI VENEZIA

  Then the small door plaque RUDGE

This is where my camera breaks down shutters
 the single lens reflex jams— pictures from that afternoon all a blur

At the end "Mr. Hall you—find me—in fragments" *Mi trovi in frammenti*

A hundred years after you I found Santa Maria dei Miracoli one afternoon—
 Renaissance jewel box among Venetian Gothic Romanesque Byzantine—
  and gave it to my students as a gift

*But the record*
            *the palimpsest—*
*a little light*
            *in great darkness—*

At the edge of the Giudecca Canal

        bitter smell of fish and the cries of sea gulls

            *dove sta memoria*

        everything

A CHURCH IN ITALY

Last summer, in a church in Italy,
    I prayed for all of you: asked not for forgiveness
        and strength, but that all the sadness of our days,

all the grief of our lives,
    all the loneliness given us be taken away
        without judgment—asked for life and light.

That was the first time in twenty-three years something
    like that happened to me. Not knowing the modern prayers,
        I fell back on the old way of ending prayer, recited:

*Glory be to the Father and to the Son*
    *and to the Holy Spirit, as it was in the beginning,*
        *is now, and ever shall be, world without end*

then dropped some lire coins in the metal offering box,
    walked through the heavily curtained doorway into the
    Mediterranean heat, into the hard traffic of the village,
                into the harsh light of the afternoon,
                        into this world without end.

Epigraph to *Italian Days & Hours*
"*The charm was, as always in Italy, in the tone and the air and the happy hazard of things ....*" From *Italian Hours* by Henry James. Edited by John Auchard (Penguin Editions, 1992).

Epigraph to Part I
*Éie mannate a spassela memoria, è festa:* "I have sent memory out for a stroll./ It's a holiday." Eugenio Cirese (1884-1955) was born in Fossalto, Molise, Italy. The quotation is from his poem "Lightning" from *Molisan Poems: Selected Poems* trans. by Luigi Bonaffini (Guernica Editions, 2000).

"At the Basilica di San Giovanni in Laterano"
The Basilica di San Giovanni in Laterano is the oldest and highest ranking of the four papal basilicas in Rome. It is the oldest basilica in the Western world. Near the entrance of the basilica, a marker announces the significance of the basilica: *Omnium urbis et orbis Ecclesiarum Mater et Caput:* "the mother and the head of all of the churches of the city and the world."

"First Morning in Sepino"
Sepino, Italy, is ancestral home to three of my grandparents. The village of 2,000 people is located in the foothills of the Matese mountain, about 20 km. south of Campobasso in the region of Molise, and approximately 108 km from Naples.

"A Sepinesi Folk Song"
On a warm, sunny morning in the summer of 1999, when I was in Sepino for the feste St. Cristina, Fra Gerardo Battista of Bari, who also was a guest at Convento S. S. Trinità, invited me to walk with him in the hills above Sepino. As we walked, Fra Gerardo began singing. When I asked him what he was singing, he told me they were old Sepinesi folksongs. When we returned to the Convento later that morning, I asked Fra Gerardo to write down the words of the songs for me. When I returned to Minnesota, I wrote to Molisano writer Giose Rimanelli (1925-2018) and asked him to help me translate the folksongs into

English. He was kind enough to do so. Giose also told me that he remembered the beautiful music of these songs.

This is one of the folksongs Fra Gerardo sang that morning. I imagine it expresses the feelings of many immigrants who left Sepino behind. I wonder if my grandparents ever sang this song after they came to America and sometimes longed for their home in Sepino?

Epigraph to Part II
Ancora imparo: "I am still learning." Found scribbled on a work sketch by Michelangelo, age 87.

"Sotteraneo"
Poscritto: When one of my friends returned from a trip to Italy, which included several days in Florence, (and with my instructions on how to gain entry to sotteraneo), he reported that sotterraneo was now permanently closed to the public—sealed by the Italian authorities because of the rapid degradation of the drawings—until some restoration plan can be developed. In addition to decomposition caused by human visitors to the non-ventilated room over the years, the discovery of bodies buried underneath the floor that were releasing gasses, were also damaging the drawings. More recently, however, and because of new technology, visitors will have virtual access to high definition images and video of Michelangelo's sotterraneo drawings at multimedia kiosk stations in San Lorenzo and at the Bargello Museum, not far away. Rumors persist, however, that there are plans to reopen sotteraneo to the public once again by 2020.

"Japanese Woman at the Cistern, Piazza della Cisterna, San Gimignano"
*"Di giugno siati in tale campagnetta*
*che viva sien corbi et arghironcelli"*
"In June a little countryside for you,
Where crows and herons are content to wile"

These are the opening lines about the month of June, taken from a sonnet cycle about the months of the year by Giacomo di

Michele (1280-1332), better known as Folgòre da San Gimignano, a contemporary of Dante. The translation is by Lorna de' Lucchi.

"Walking to San Miniato al Monte on Sunday Morning"
St. Minias, first Christian martyr of Florence, lived a hermit's life, surviving executions from stoning and being fed to lions. Eventually beheaded, St. Minias, legend has it, waded across the Arno while carrying his head so that he could return to his beloved home, on one of the  highest hills in Florence.

The inscription on the wall at the foot of the staircase that leads to San Miniato al Monte is from Dante's Purgatorio XII. It is one of thirty such inscriptions placed throughout Florence.

> to ascend the mount,
> Where seated is the Church that lordeth it
>
> O'er the well-guided, above Rubiconte,
> The bold abruptness of the ascent is broken
> By stairways that were made there in the age,
> When still were safe the ledger and the stave.

"Visiting Pound's Apartment in Venice"
The inscription above Ezra Pound's apartment at Calle Quierini 252, Venice, reads:

IN HIS UNDYING LOVE FOR VENICE
EZRA POUND
GIANT OF POETRY
LIVED IN THIS HOUSE FOR A HALF-CENTURY

THE TOWN OF VENICE

*But the record*
> *the palimpsest—*
*a little light*
> *in great darkness—*
>> —From "Canto CXVI"

*dove sta memoria:* "where love stays." In "Canto LVXXI," Pound quotes Guido Cavalcanti, 13th century poet from Florence.

## ACKNOWLEDGMENTS

To the editors of the following publications, where some of these poems first appeared, sometimes in earlier versions: mille grazie!

*Flurry:* "At the Basilica di San Giovanni in Laterano"
*Giornali St. Cristina:* "via St. Cristina"
*North Dakota Quarterly:* "Innocent Traveler"
*University of Windsor Review:* "A Church in Italy"
*VIA Voices in Italian Americana:* "Wide Awake in Rome"
*23 Poems* (Red Dragonfly Press): "We Arrive in the Village"
*Beyond Borders: An Anthology of New Writing from Manitoba, Minnesota, Saskatchewan, and the Dakotas* (Turnstone Press & New Rivers Press): "A Photograph of You at the House of the Dead in Ascona"
*Holding on for Dear Life* (Spoon River Poetry Press): "Found in Translation: My Hotel Room in Rome"; "Rome, Morning"

I am grateful to an anonymous donor who supported the publication of this book. I also want to thank Andrew Jones & Angela Jones for their assistance and support during the making this book—sempre amici.

Tante grazie: Padre Agostino, Fra Bernadine, Sheila Coghill, Luciana Iamartino, Patrizia Iamartino, Tom Koontz, Angela Mancinelli, Maria Grazia Tagliaferri, Antonio Tammaro, and Padre Vittorio.

## COLOPHON

The text is set in Cardo, an Old Style typeface designed by David J. Perry in 2002. The font is inspired by the Italian printer Aldus Pius Manutius, who founded the Aldine Press in Venice in 1494 and first issued books in the small octavo size featuring the first use of italics. The Aldine Press was located in the *Thermae* in the Sestiere di San Polo on the campo Sant'Agostin which is now *civico numero 2343 San Polo* on the *calle della Chiesa*.